M000160015

SLICK AF: THE AFIB RABBIT HOLE

Uncovering the Truth About *Paroxysmal Atrial Fibrillation*

by Kristian Davidson

TEASER

Accompany me through the entire process of a first-time *Paroxysmal Atrial Fibrillation* diagnosis. How did I get this condition? What kind of *tests* were required? What were my *treatment options*?

I listened to them all and disagreed. Then I found the answer in a most random place, at just the right moment, and the pieces of the puzzle fit together.

The *why* may be shocking. The *truth* is so simple. The *cure* is so cheap. Was I almost a *victim* of a profiteering western medical system? I find it hard to believe the *doctors* didn't know, but could this rabbit hole go even deeper?

FOREWORD

I am not a doctor and I am in no way, shape, or form giving any health advice in this book. This is my personal journey which lead me to my own conclusions that, in fact, *cured* me of lifelong debilitating migraines and a diagnosis of paroxysmal atrial fibrillation. I no longer suffer from these ailments and my goal is to share the experience of that journey with anyone who may be interested in my story.

CONTENTS

Title Page 1

Teaser 3

Foreword 4

First time 7

Immediate Care Clinic 11

Emergency Room 12

Cardioversion 13

Prescriptions 15

Symbol of Hope 16

Side Effects 19

Think About It 22

Primary Care Physician 24

Ultrasound 26

Stress Test 27

Something Stinks 28

Heart Specialist 30

New Doctor 31

Making Changes 32

Migraine Season 33

Migraine Doctors 35

Migraine Relief 36

Second Time 37

Eureka! 39

Magnesium 41

Lightning & Thunder 43

Telling My Doctor 45

Where is Our Magnesium? 46

3rd Time's a Charm 48

Final Thoughts 49

FIRST TIME

The first time it happened... I thought I was dying. It was just a normal day like every other day in my life. I was dead tired at work, working through it. I worked every day and my job was not as easy as it should be due to an overbearing, mildly retarded, clueless but arrogant boss. There are only three of us on the crew but she made sure we did the work of twelve employees every day. Working hard was normal to me so I knew she was burning us out, but I really didn't mind. That was just the way I was; a hard worker.

For the last three months, however, I was burning my candle at both ends. I did what I did at work every day and then came home to my fixer-upper house that seemed to have an endless punch list of repairs to complete on my "night shift" and weekends. Every time I noticed something, I wrote it down on the punch list so I could get things done faster. The house needed a lot of work.

So I was working day and night for three months with little sleep. The last two weeks or so, before the incident, I was getting so much done that it gave me the ambition to do more. I gave up food and water for the cause and subsisted solely on cigarettes and Mountain Dew with a sporadic double cheeseburger from McDonalds now and then. I just kept working. I didn't really care about anything else because I was seeing more and more progress being made on the house.

I left work on Friday at six pm for the weekend just like I always did. I knew that I would be working non-stop on the house for the next couple of days so I stopped at the gas station and picked up two cases of Mountain Dew and a few extra packs of smokes to get

7

me through it.

I worked on the house all weekend and made enough progress to justifiably stop early on Sunday evening. I wanted to catch up on some sleep before work the next day. Unfortunately, I drank too much caffeine all weekend and I couldn't sleep.

I tossed and turned all night in the flickering light of the television. I was listening to some show but had my head turned away from it's light until something caught my attention and urged me to look at the screen. I would turn my head and watch part of a show and then turn back away and try to sleep.

Over and over and over. Next thing you know, my alarm starts beeping and *suddenly*... I'm finally tired enough to go to sleep just in time to get up and go to work. I guess the caffiene finally wore off.

I hit the snooze button several times at five minute intervals until the clock dictated that I had to get up or I would be late to work. I got up out of bed, went through my morning routine, and locked up the house.

As soon as I got in the car, I cracked open a cold Mountain Dew and lit my first cigarette. That's how I started every new day and it's always worked well for me.

I drove to work and went right into satisfying the ridiculous demands of my boss. She started texting me with tasks to complete before I was even on the clock as usual. I never respond to texts or calls from work before 7am. One would think she would eventually catch on to that at some point.

It's been five and a half years now and Ive been doing it that way since I realized that she, and the owners of the company, did not appreciate our commitment or loyalty nor showed any graciousness or gratitude for the sheer volumes of work that our crew accomplished on a daily basis. If we had worked for anyone else, we would be seen as superheroes and that's the bottom line truth.

Our upper management paraded themselves around as Christians, praying about everything and trying to share their faith with their employees. It was obvious that they were hypocrites. They did not practice any faith in their employees, or gratitude, or forgiveness. They were more like Judas than Jesus; always scheming behind our backs.

I saw that plain as day by the way they treated the people around them and the way they falsified and deleted documents before government inspections. That's a whole other story though. I never did feel that my job was very secure there so I worked hard to show them that I was worth keeping. My work speaks for itself wherever I go..

That Monday morning went as usual up until lunch time. Since I was so very tired from being awake all night, I decided to take a nap during my 30-minute lunch break. I set my alarm for 30 minutes and actually fell asleep laying on my back.

Went the alarm went off, I sat up kind of fast and leaned forward to stand up. As soon as I stood up, my heart started skipping beats and acting all crazy. That has never happened to me before.

A normal heart beat has a two-thump rhythm and loops into a cadence whether it be fast or slow. Mine felt like the two thumps were separated and both thumps were just doing their own thing. They weren't working together.

My first thought was that I was having a heart attack but every time I'd seen someone having a heart attack on TV, they would grab their chest like they were in great pain. I was not having any pain at all. Aside from the crazy town parade beating in my chest, everything else felt normal.

So I decided to tell my boss that I had to go home. She was understanding due to the circumstances and I left the property wondering if I should go to the emergency room or if my heart would go back to normal by itself. Then I remembered that there is an immediate care clinic that accepted my insurance about mile from my house so I stopped there on my way home.

IMMEDIATE CARE CLINIC

I went up to the desk and told the lady that my heart was beating weird and she told me to go straight into a small room where the nurse immediately checked my pulse and then hooked me up to an electrocardiogram machine to confirm that my heart was out of rhythm and to determine which *type* of out-of-rhythm it was.

The nurse then told me that I should take the ECG printout to the emergency room right away. She very much expressed urgency to get there as soon as possible. I left the clinic with the printout thinking, even more now, that I was going to die.

Since I was just down the road from my house, I went home and told my son and daughter what was happening. My son drove us to the emergency room at a hospital 30 miles away because I had little faith in the hospital in my home town based on other peoples' experiences there.

EMERGENCY ROOM

Upon arrival at the emergency room I, again, was pushed to the front of the line and given a room and another, more detailed, ECG. They confirmed that I was experiencing Paroxysmal Atrial Fibrillation. The *Paroxysmal* means that it is not an ongoing condition, but a random one.

They also said that, now that I have had this once, I will continue to have this problem throughout the remainder of my life. They said it will never go away.

They wheeled me from the ER into the heart care section of the hospital and hooked me up to an IV solution which they told me was needed to hydrate my blood. I hate needles, but I allowed it.

They also took some blood samples to check into why this was suddenly happening to me. Then I hung out with my kids for a long time, my heart still going crazy, while I waited for them to do anything more. We watched a few episodes of Criminal Minds or CSI or something. I don't really remember.

CARDIOVERSION

When the heart doctor finally came back, he said all my tests came back normal and there shouldn't be any problems,... yet there we were. Due to everything being normal on my tests and the fact that I was "too young" to have heart issues, the doctor said that they could use a defibrillator to shock my heart back into rythm. Supposedly this would fix the irregular heartbeat and I would be able to leave the hospital cured. There was a catch though.

When they shock my heart, they said it might stop my heart and they may not be able to bring me back. So there's a risk to the procedure but multiple heart doctors in the room assured me that the risk was extremely minimal and that they didn't expect any complications because I was so young and in good physical shape. I agreed to the procedure and then the other shoe fell.

Apparently shocking a person's heart is so unimaginably painful that they wanted to put me under anesthesia to perform the treatment. I had already taken so many needles, what was one more? I agreed to that too.

They moved me into another room with about 5-8 doctors all focused on me. They strapped me to the table and injected the shot into my IV tube so I was at least relieved that I didn't get another needle-hole in my arm.

After the injection, I faded out. I have no idea what happened during the procedure. I just remember waking up confused for a few minutes while the room stopped spinning. As soon as I regained my faculties, I felt my heart was back into a normal two-thump rhythm.

They wheeled my whole bed back into the private room, hooked me up to a bunch of machines, and told me I had to stay there for a while so they could keep an eye on my stats. I felt much better with my heart beating normally again and joked around with my kids while we waited.

PRESCRIPTIONS

When the doctor came back in, he gave me a prescription for some blood thinners and told me I need to take them because when the heart doesn't pump like it should, there is an area where blood pools. When blood is stagnant in a pool, it may begin to clot. If a piece of the clot breaks off and flows into the bloodstream, I could have a stroke. Again, they assured me that the risk was very minimal so not to worry about it too much but to take the pills "just to make sure".

He wrote out a second prescription for pills that will control the rate at which my heart beats to prevent my heart from beating out of control again. He said I may need to take these pills for the rest of my life. I heard him say that but,.. that was not going to happen. If I have to take a pill every day to stay alive, I think I would just rather let nature take its course. Besides, my heart was fine now. I probably wouldn't need the pills anyway.

I always fill my prescriptions and then put the pills in a drawer until they expire. I don't trust the profiteering western medical system; least of all, the pharmaceutical industry. I just don't take pills of any kind into my body unless absolutely necessary. These pills would get the same amount of suspicion and avoidance as any other pill I've encountered..

SYMBOL OF HOPE

The doctor told me that I should make an appointment with a heart specialist and gave me a referral to a "good one". He said I was good to go and as I walked out of the room, completely cured of an irregular heart rhythm, the entire staff of doctors, nurses, receptionists and others were watching me leave with genuine, big smiles on their faces.

There were so many people looking directly at me. The ones way in the back or down the hallways were moving there necks as people got in the way to keep their gaze on me. I think the doctor who escorted us out of the room saw the look of confusion on my face as I realized, right in front of him, that everyone was looking and smiling at me. I slowly turned away from all of the staring, smiling people toward the doctor who was holding the door open for us.

As my gaze approached the doctor's eyes, he bashfully looked down away from me and said softly, "It's very rare that someone comes into this part of the hospital..." he paused, then looked back up at me, "and *walks* out again."

I looked back out at the smiling people but this time I saw the people who were *not* looking at me. They were patients and visitors who didn't even notice me. Most were elderly and hooked up to tubes and wires with elderly visitors pushing them around in wheelchairs or sitting silently beside their beds. I realized I was standing in den of great sadness.

I felt his words and those smiles in my soul and they lifted my heart. It was a real, physical manifestation of hope that hung thick in the air around me, but *they* were all looking at me like it was emanating from my pores and filling the entire space. I felt like a conduit for some kind of energy that was flowing through me to be a symbol of hope to all of those weary souls who toiled in a place of sadness and loss; almost like I was placed there for that exact purpose.

There may have been one person in that group of people who cares for heart patients day in and day out. He or she experiences sadness and loss with every single person she comes in contact with throughout her work day. Maybe the negative vibrations were wearing her down and God's plan was to use me to lift her back up with a success story which may have been all she needed to reinvigorate her ambition to help people. The person she may help one day could be the person that changes everything. Maybe my being there changed everything.

I don't really know how it all fits together into a plan but when I walked out of there *cured*, while all those people's smiles warmed the room in front of me, I was part of something that happened to a lot of people. Something happened to them, through me, that I was not responsible for. I had only met a handful of them. It certainly felt like a plan from someone greater than me. I never told anyone about that before.

It was only a few split seconds between opening the door to the room, the doctors comment, the smiles, the sadness, and walking out into the parking lot to leave. It was only a few seconds for *all* of that to happen. I notice things like that often. Time seems to slow down for me so I can see all the details as if I am reading a sign that tells me I am still a part of the plan. It happened so fast that

17

I don't think my kids saw any of it right there in front of their eyes.

We left the hospital at around 11pm and arrived home around 11:30. I set up a scheduled text message on my phone app to be sent at 7:00am to tell my boss I need the day off. That's how I called in to work. Coolest job I ever had. Anyway, I was so tired, I just passed out and slept through the next day.

SIDE EFFECTS

I was exhausted from all the work I was doing with no sleep and no food for weeks. I just had my heart tazed and I'm sure that needs to heal. I woke up late at night the next day and sent my son to fill my prescriptions for me and started taking those as the doctor ordered.

The pills scared me a little because one of the side effects said "death" right on the information sheet. I didn't read that until after I followed the instructions on the bottle and popped the first pills as directed. One would think that if the first side effect is listed as "death" and the second side effect is "stroke" followed by "stroke up to six months after discontinued use" of the pills... I'm thinking *that* medication deserves a big, black skull and bones symbol right on the bottle. So, *great*, I already took one of each.

I didn't notice anything at first, but I guess the heart rhythm pills have to build up in your system. After they did, I found out how they work. My heart used to work normally. When I exerted myself, it would beat faster. When I rested, it would beat slower. The rhythm-control pills took control of the speed of my heart and kept it at one speed *all the time* depending on the dosage.

The dosage I was receiving caused me to feel like my heart was racing when I was resting and when I tried to exert myself, it could not keep up with me and I would find myself pausing to catch my breath.

The longer I was on the pills, the less amount of energy I had to get out of bed. I had to stop on every fifth step of my 15-step staircase to rest because I was out of breath. I literally ran marathons all day long, every day at work including multiple staircases. Getting up the stairs at my house has never been a challenge. So... this was really weird and unacceptable to me and it was absolutely the medication that made me feel like that.

The other medication was a blood thinner that I later saw on one of those legal-type infomercials on late night TV. However they said this one was only temporary for a week or two to prevent a blood clot from any pooling that may have happened. It made me feel a little bit lighter but that was about it. Same as an aspirin.

One of the warnings on this medication was that if I cut myself, I could bleed to death because my blood will not clot while using it. The doctor even told me not to cut myself when he wrote the prescription as well as the pharmacist stressed that to my son when he picked it up for me.

I had to wait a week or more to get an appointment with a Primary Care Physician and went back to work while on the medications. I couldn't do much of anything at work for a while. I mostly just shuffled around the shop and organized things. I swept the floor but I had trouble bending down to use the dust pan without getting out of breath and light-headed.

Although my coworkers were sympathetic, I didn't think the crew would let me be *lazy* for too long. We had a very demanding job. I had to start thinking about what I might have to do if I were to get fired. The anxiety and worry started to pile up on top of me. What if I was going to be an invalid the rest of my life? How will I continue to support myself and my family if I can no longer work?

The self-negativity began to swirl around me and, yet, I still felt somewhat detached from it. I kept hearing a voice of hope in my heart saying things like "you are in very good shape from working hard all those years" and "the doctors said you are too young to have heart problems". The hope began to drown out the negative thoughts and I decided I was going to learn all there was to know about my condition so I can *know my enemy*.

THINK ABOUT IT

I started with Google and legitimate foundational western medicine. I looked at how the heart pumps blood, that electrical signals open and close valves, and studied what a heart actually is. I didn't really find anything useful to explain my condition but I learned a lot over the course of a few days with a search engine.

I actually learned so much that I kept seeing the same information in multiple publications. I figured that was pretty much it as far as the physical aspects of the heart and none of it really lead me to anything that might help other than knowing that electrical signals open and close the valves and pump the heart but nobody knows how or why.

Think about that for a minute. In their own literature, they *admit* that they do *not* understand how or why electrical signals misfire to cause AFib. Think about that statement alone while they are trying to convince you that the solution is to burn off pieces of your heart that send and receive electrical signals.

Think about that when they have already burned off pieces of your heart and are now trying to convince you that you need a pacemaker because the last procedure damaged your signal receptors and your heart will never beat properly again unless they install the pacemaker to solve the problem.

Think about that. They do *not* understand why my heart is doing what it is doing but they want to *damage* my heart to fix it? It just

22

doesn't make any sense to me.

PRIMARY CARE PHYSICIAN

I went to an appointment with my primary care physician who I just picked out of a list online. I never go to doctors so I didn't have one at the time. I picked a female doctor because male doctors tend to be condescending. Unfortunately, I picked the wrong one.

She started our first meeting by looking over my file without engaging me first. When she finally looked up at me, she snarled her disapproval at the ER doctors who shocked my heart and said *she* would have admitted me to the hospital and controlled my heart with medication until it went back to its normal rhythm on its own.

I did not like the sound of that at all. I thought those ER doctors did the right thing and I was very happy with how they treated me there. Had they admitted me to the hospital I, and all those other people, would have missed that split-second momentary rush of hope that affected us all. It's moments like those that live in our hearts forever. She is telling me I should not have experienced that profound moment in time that no *man* could have planned.

After telling her that I felt fine and had reservations about the medications I was prescribed, she said I felt fine *because* of the medications and to keep taking them. However I had already established as a *fact*, that the medication was affecting me in a negative and unusual manner. Who would know better; me knowing what I feel in my own body from direct experience or the person who was looking through the pharmaceutical database right in front of me?

She was literally matching my symptoms and the thoughts that I expressed with a database where the only option available for treatment is a pharmaceutical product. There were no other options anywhere within her field of view. Nothing. That was the farthest extent of her medical knowledge; the ability to search *one* database really well. This stunned me. Grade School children could have done her job that day.

She then *ordered* me to continue both medications *indefinitely* and she would call in refill prescriptions for me. She also told me to set up an *ultrasound* and a *stress test* before I could see the *heart specialist.* After seeing this drug dealer, I decided to stop taking all of my pills right then and there. She was obviously a pharmaceutical salesperson and did not have my best interests in mind.

I decided to go ahead and keep my other appointments because they came with test results that I needed to know followed by a meeting with a heart specialist to explain the results to me but I was very skeptical of the process from this point on.

ULTRASOUND

The *ultrasound* was not a bad experience. I had to take my shirt off and lay on a padded exam table, sometimes on my back and sometimes on my side to get a complete 3D image of my heart. The ultrasound would determine if there were any physical abnormalities with my heart such as a misaligned valve or any operational issues with the flow of my blood, or possibly a defect or growth.

I was in a room alone with a very pretty nurse around 10 years younger than me. She turned the lights off so she could see the computer screen better which made me feel much more at ease. She rubbed the gel lubricant all over my chest and stomach which felt amazing. I've been single and untouched for over a decade and she had such warm hands. I might go back and have it checked again someday.

She explained everything she was doing and let me watch my heart beating on the monitor as she snapped screenshots of my heart measurements. I really enjoyed this part of the process. When it was over, I asked the nurse if she had noticed anything alarming during the scan that I should know about.

She responded that she was not allowed to say anything to me about the results because they have to be interpreted by the heart specialist. So I left there feeling good but without any more answers.

STRESS TEST

The next step was the *stress test* which consisted of being hooked up to an electrocardiogram with many more leads than the immediate care clinic or the ER used on me. This one is more detailed. After getting all wired up to the machine, the nurse told me to run on a treadmill that will gradually get faster and more inclined as the test goes on while she watched and analyzed the data on a computer screen.

Due to my decision to stop my medication a while ago, my heart was speeding up and slowing down like it should and I was able to outrun the test because I really *was* in good shape. I did not become out of breath or ask to stop. She stopped the test, after about 15 minutes, when she got all the data she needed. If I had been on the rhythm medication, I could not have done this test for 30 seconds.

After the stress test, the stress test doctor came into the room and looked over the data for a few minutes and declared that everything looked good. There were no anomalies or mis-fires, or skipped beats or anything. He said my heart was working exactly as it should and that made me feel a lot better but I wondered what he may have said to me if I *had* been taking my medication as directed and failed right at the beginning of the stress test.

SOMETHING STINKS

I was starting to see a pattern where I was getting poisoned and then passed from doctor to doctor and my insurance company was paying them off one after another. I didn't feel like I was being duped because I know I needed the results of all of these tests to know what was happening to me, but something wasn't right.

I just kept thinking what they might have said to me if I had listened to them and the medication had interfered with the tests. I would have to go see more specialists and pay out more money. The scam was getting much clearer as it potentially included more doctors, more procedures, and more payouts.

What could I do but continue my research? The whole experience was starting to stink of corruption and it all started with pharmaceutical products that were disabling my body by design.

I started searching deeper into *Atrial Fibrillation*. Electrical signals that tell the valves to open and close are controlled by a mechanism that controls their rhythm. When the signals are not operating properly, they can be *forced* to operate properly with medications.

When drugs don't work, the next option is *ablation*. That is where they stick a laser into your chest and burn off the nerves that send or receive the signals. However if this procedure is done and it doesn't fix the problem, they will have destroyed the signalling process and you will then be given a pacemaker attached to your heart for the rest of your life.

...and they make *you* pay them for the pacemaker that you need after *THEY* damaged your heart. Remember in their own literature, they state that they do *not* know what they are doing! Nice process, huh?

It seemed like the more "treatments" you get for this condition, the more damage is done until your heart is disabled, life is pretty much over, and you are broke and on disability. At which point, there is no more hope to cure this dis-ease because you will be saddled by hundreds of thousands of dollars, possibly millions, in medical debt that you can never pay off because you can not work due to being hooked up to a pacemaker for the rest of your life.

I decided I was not going to let this process go that far. I suspected that this happened to me because I overtaxed my body. I really over-did it and I knew *that* to be true. Sometimes you just have to go with what you know to be true and disregard the theories and doctrines of others. I *know* I burned myself out.

HEART SPECIALIST

I had to wait over a month to see the heart specialist. When I finally got in to see him, he went over all of my test results with me and concluded that there is nothing wrong with me at all. He asked me if I was still taking both of my prescriptions and I lied to him and said yes.

As soon as I said yes, he shook his head and said that I am much to young to be on either one of those medications and directed me to stop them immediately. He gave me a clean bill of heart health and instructed me to see my Primary Care Physician in 30 days for a follow-up.

NEW DOCTOR

When I called to make the follow-up appointment with the worthless PCP that I had picked myself earlier, her receptionist told me that she was not taking any more appointments because she was moving out of state. I was very relieved at the sound of that and started looking for a new PCP to replace her.

I decided that I did not like the hospital or the ER in my hometown but I was not opposed to having a PCP in town if he or she was in a private building away from the hospital. I found one and made an appointment.

The month went by fast with no further heart issues. I went to the appointment and told him everything was good. He checked my pulse and listened to my heart and agreed with me and that was the end of it.

MAKING CHANGES

I made the decision to slow down at work so I don't overexert myself again. Especially since they didn't really deserve my best after the way we were being treated at work anyway. I stopped working on my house for a while and just rested on the weekends and hung out with my kids.

I stopped drinking caffiene-laced Mountain Dew and switched to an occasional non-caffiene soda. The bulk of my hydration was replaced with real, organic fruit juices and purified water. I also replaced my fast food diet with fresh fruits and vegetables, rice, and wild-caught alaskan salmon as my meat source.

I still only buy sour dough bread to this day because I learned that it is the only bread that comes with positive health benefits while all other bread has negative effects. I quit smoking for about 3 weeks but then slowly started smoking again. Even so, I was feeling healthier than ever before in my life just by changing my diet.

Unfortunately, the months flew by and I stopped thinking about my heart altogether. I even gave up on my research to cure myself. I started drinking Mountain Dew to excess again. I went back to fast food.

MIGRAINE SEASON

Nothing had happened for so long that I felt everything was back to normal. Then I got one of my regular seasonal migraines. I would get them every year when the seasons change from hot to cold in the fall and again when they change from cold to hot in the spring.

They would usually last about 3 weeks and are excruciatingly painful. I've been getting them for probably 20 years, twice a year like clockwork. I usually save all of my vacation time at work to use when the migraines put me out of commission for days at a time. I called it *Migraine Season*.

The migraines would get so painful that I had to squeeze myself into a ball and scream into a pillow for hours on end. I can't imagine what my neighbors thought of us when they heard it. Sometimes one of my kids would rub my neck in just the right way on the right spot and the pain would diminish for a few brief moments but when they stopped rubbing, the pain came roaring back.

I am very grateful to my children, who are adults now, for helping me through some very dark and painful times. They always tried to help me any way they could. I truly don't deserve them.

While in the throes of a migraine, I couldn't see. As long as I was in complete darkness, my eyes would be open but all I could see were flashing colors like arcs sporadically shooting from one side of my view to the other. If someone walked into the room and turned the light on, the colors would be replaced with bright, white light arcs and the pain level would shoot up a hundredfold which would make me scream even louder and shove my face further into the pillow to block out the light.

MIGRAINE DOCTORS

I went to the "doctors" for it, in the beginning, and they could never figure it out. They always told me there was nothing wrong with me. I had CAT scans and X-rays and everything and got no answers from any of them. I stopped believing that doctors were smarter than me a long time ago when they began to look at me like I was using "migraines" as an excuse to get opiates.

I know that look very well because my ex-wife was an opiate seeker. Unfortunately for their theory, narcotic pills make the migraines worse so I've never asked for them nor accepted any for the migraines. When I needed to try one, I already knew where to get them. I did not need a doctor for that.

MIGRAINE RELIEF

I've tried acetaminophen, naproxen, aspirin, ibuprofen, norco, vicodin, and percocet; all the usual pain relievers. They can all take the edge off the pain and dull it slightly, but nothing would make them go away. The narcotic pills actually make the pain intensify so I never used those for migraines after the first trial with each kind.

The ones that helped the most were the headache pills with a mixture of acetominophin, aspirin, and caffiene. I took superman doses and even that did not help very much but it worked better than all the rest.

There was only one way that I could stop a migraine in it's tracks, but there was a price to pay when I did it. I found out that there was a pill that will make them stop within 10 minutes or so.

Pseudoephedrine worked every time I tried it but the problem with those is that the very moment the pill wears off, the migraine will come roaring back with the vengeance of hell itself and after taking one of those pills, nothing else will help until the migraine is finished with its cycle and I black out from the pain. I only used those as a last resort, if ever. The backlash was *that* bad.

SECOND TIME

So back to my story,... I was a few days into Migraine Season which is right about the time the pain levels start going off the chart. I also caught a cold or the flu or something on top of the migraines and was suffering through both ailments. The migraines were so bad that I considered using the pseudoephedrine and rationalized it by telling myself it would help with the cold as well. I talked myself into taking the pill to end the migraine and to help me breathe better. I took the pill.

Ten minutes later, the migraine calmed down as expected and I was just starting to come back from the pain when my heart started mis-firing again. It had been about nine months since my first AFib incident. I couldn't believe it was happening again. I wanted nothing more than to go to sleep since I had already been up for hours with the migraine and was completely worn out from pain and weak from sickness.

I did not get to go to sleep. My son took me to the ER for my AFib again. Even though my heart was acting up, the pain from the migraine was gone which left me in semi-good spirits at the ER while the nurses hooked me up to the machines again.

When the nurse put the IV in my arm this time, I asked her what was in the IV bag because I wanted to know how they were going to fix me this time. I might be too sick and weak to get shocked again. She told me it was just saline to help rehydrate my blood. When she walked out of the room, I turned to look at the bag and I read the label. It said Magnesium not saline. I thought that was odd but I was too weak to think any more about it.

After all the tests were done, they put me back on the same two medications as before and sent me home with my heart still not functioning. They said it would get better on its own if I just take the pills. So I took the first dose from the doctors right there and then we left the hospital with two more prescriptions of death pills.

EUREKA!

When I got home, I crawled into bed and immediately continued researching my condition. Why was this happening to me again? I didn't overwork myself this time. It must have been that pseudoephedrine pill I took. It had to be. But I'd taken those many times before in my life and have never had a problem with them.

I reasoned that there must be some underlying condition in my body that has weakened me and I've become fragile enough that my nerves stop firing properly under the slightest of circumstances. I had electrical issues. That's what it felt like anyway.

Within a few hours, I had read many more articles and publications on AFib, nerve damage, and heart functions. I got tired of reading and started clicking on YouTube videos of other people with heart conditions.

I watched them one after another hoping for something that would tell me why this was happening to me. I did not want to live like this where I am afraid to do anything that might set off my heart condition. ...and then I found it!

The answer to WHY this was happening was summed up in a one-line comment, from some random person, under a YouTube video that I was listening to while reading the comments.

The person said simply "100% of ALL AFib cases are caused by a magnesium deficiency." As soon as I read that comment, I remembered looking at the IV drip they gave me at the ER. That was when it hit me right in the face. They *KNEW*.

They *knew* what was wrong with me the whole time and they tried to trap me into their pharmaceutical scam. The very first thing they did to me upon arrival with "AFib" was to put me on a magnesium drip... BOTH times I went to the ER! Those lying bastards *KNEW* the whole time!

MAGNESIUM

I started watching videos on magnesium and magnesium deficiency and wouldn't you know it?.. I had all the symptoms they listed for a magnesium deficiency. ALL of them! The more I watched and read online, the more I was convinced my problem was solved.

My son was going to go pick up my prescriptions at the pharmacy so I got on the pharmacy website and started looking at magnesium supplements. Some people were saying that magnesium oxide gives them gas and magnesium citrate gives you stomach aches and everyone had their own opinion on what type of Magnesium to take as a supplement.

I found two kinds of magnesium on the pharmacy's website that looked promising to me. There was a slow-release magnesium that I thought would give me what I need slowly throughout the day and then they had a store brand triple-magnesium complex that had three different kinds mixed together into one pill. I asked my son to pick both of them up while he was there.

As soon as he got home with the magnesium supplements, I took one of the slow-release pills hoping that it would help me while I slept that night, but I waited an hour or so and my heart was still beating out of control and I was not feeling any better and I couldn't sleep.

I then reasoned that if I have such a high level of deficiency, it would be acceptable to take more than the recommended dose. I

41

took one of the triple complex pills and drank a bottle of water. I started watching a movie on Netflix and tried to relax and wait for something to happen.

LIGHTNING & THUNDER

About an hour into the movie, I was just sitting there hoping it would work and not really paying much attention to the movie. Suddenly out of nowhere, it felt like lightning hit me in the head, not painful, but a noticeable electrical shock that came out of nowhere and struck the remnants of the migraine pain that I thought had actually gone away.

It was like a tingly shocky feeling around all of the parts where the migraine had been the most painful and what was left of the pain disintegrated in a matter of moments into short bursts of tiny electrical arcs all over my skull and then it was gone.

I've never had a migraine *just go away* like that. I prayed for 20 years for that to happen every time I had a migraine and never before had that ever happened. The migraine was totally gone from my head.

A few minutes later, like a thunder cloud in my chest, I felt a rumble and then a shock-snap like my heart was just electrically shocked and the beats snapped back into sync with each other. It was so sudden that it took me by surprise and I actually jumped up to a standing position on my mattress and checked my pulse. My heart was back in perfect rhythm. I literally ran down the hall and barged into my son's room and told him it worked! The magnesium worked!

I took the next day off from work, since I had already scheduled the vacation time due to the ER trip and the migraines. I spent the

43

whole day re-watching and re-visiting magnesium information because I wanted to know *how* it fixed my migraines as well.

It turns out that one of the symptoms of a magnesium deficiency is migraines. All those years I spent in torturous pain were caused by the very same thing that was causing my heart to malfunction. What a revelation. I immediately stopped taking the prescribed medication and started taking the triple magnesium complex pill every day.

TELLING MY DOCTOR

After a few days, I attended an appointment with my doctor as a follow-up to my second ER visit. I told him what I discovered and that I was now taking a magnesium supplement every day and that I stopped taking my prescriptions.

I expected him to throw a fit and tell me how I'm wrong and that I need to be taking their medicines but he didn't. He just looked at me like a child with his hand caught in the cookie jar and said, "ok... I don't see any problem with that"...

What kind of response was that from a doctor? I now think they ALL know about this and they are not allowed to tell people. He had nothing more to say so I thanked him for his time and left.

WHERE IS OUR MAGNESIUM?

Another thing I learned about having a magnesium deficiency is that magnesium used to be readily available in our food but that is no longer the case because of mineral-poor soil and food processing techniques. We can no longer rely on our food as a significant source of magnesium.

Whether that be by design or by fate, I don't know but it sure looks like such a deficiency can cause all different kinds of ailments in different people which in turn creates a market for unneeded pharmaceutical products and procedures. Some of my research even touched on other nerve-related diseases being caused by a lack of magnesium.

If in fact they've removed it from our diet on purpose, it is a very strategic move because extra magnesium is stored in our bone marrow. If there is a lack of it in the gut or the bloodstream, your body will pull reserves of it from the bone marrow.

Magnesium is used by every single cell in the human body to repair cell damage. It is also an electrolyte which stabilizes electrical signals from cell to cell. Being an electrolyte, it can be expelled with persperation as you become more active. The problem with magnesium is that once you have depleted most all of your magnesium, you start to have electrical failures as a warning to replenish your electrolytes. If you continue to ignore those warnings like I did, you will have to live with migraines and irregular heartbeats, or AFib.

The doctors did test my magnesium levels and found them to be normal, but the tests that they do can only measure what is currently in your bloodstream. It doesn't tell you that what is in your bloodstream is a regulated amount based on your body pulling from reserves to keep a constant amount in the bloodstream. And they can *not* test for how much you have in reserve.

So here's the most important part. When you have used up all of your reserves, it takes approximately six months to a year to begin to replenish the reserves in your bone marrow. In my case, being such an active person, very little of any new magnesium was going back into my reserves. I was most likely sweating most of it back out.

Even taking the supplements and having a healthy supply of magnesium in the blood will not quickly cure me of AFib because magnesium is absorbed so slowly into the bone marrow. I learned that the hard way with a third and final episode of AFib.

3RD TIME'S A CHARM

I 'd been taking my supplements for quite a while and did not feel even a hint of an irregular heartbeat for a long time. About a year and half after my second ER visit, I had slipped back into my fast food and caffeine diet, stopped taking the supplements for a few weeks and thought I was invincible again.

I was sitting down watching a movie before bed one night and I decided to get up and get a drink. I got up too fast and got a head rush and my heart mis-fired into AFib again. Luckily I knew exactly what was wrong with me.

I took one of the triple magnesium complex pills and drank a full bottle of purified water and within an hour or so, my heart snapped right back into sync. No trip to the emergency room. No insurance payments to pharmaceutical sales reps pretending to be doctors. No more.

That was the last time I had any heart problems and I solved it myself in less than an hour. I now take my supplement every day and I try to stay hydrated at all times. I no longer work for the people who drove me into this condition. I also have not had a single migraine since the very first dose of magnesium. I have truly been *blessed* by knowledge in that respect.

FINAL THOUGHTS

I will be okay now, but it deeply saddens me that many people with this and similar dis-eases will not take the time to do their own research and rely solely on the fakirs we hold up as medical professionals.

It seems to me that all of the information is actually out there to cure most anything. If you decide to ignore that information and place your health or life in someone else's hands, you will get exactly what they have been indoctrinated to give you.

It was an almost three year journey for me to figure it all out and to get the pendulum to swing back the other way. The lying doctors and their profiteering medical procedures scared me into finding an alternative.

I will not live my life with a machine that controls the beat of my heart or allow somebody to burn pieces of my heart without asking some questions and checking their answers. But that's just me. This story should scare the crap out of everyone. I was lucky. I found the 2-cent magnesium pill and exited their matrix.

The End